EDGE BOOKS

BEHIND THE SCENES WITH THE PROS

BEHIND THE SCENES OF PRO HOCKEY

BY ERIN NICKS

CAPSTONE PRESS
a capstone imprint

Edge Books are published by Capstone Press,
1710 Roe Crest Drive, North Mankato, Minnesota 56003
www.mycapstone.com

Library of Congress Cataloging-in-Publication Data

Library of Congress Cataloging-in-Publication Data is available on the Library of Congress website.
ISBN: 978-1-5435-5426-7 (library hardcover)
ISBN: 978-1-5435-5920-0 (paperback)
ISBN: 978-1-5435-5431-1 (eBook PDF)

Editorial Credits

Bradley Cole, editor; Craig Hinton, designer; Ryan Gale, production specialist

Photo Credits

AP Images: Gene J. Puskar, cover, Al Diaz/The Miami Herald, 19; Icon Sportswire: Jeanine Leech, 15, Matthew Pearce, 17, Patrick Gorski, 23; iStockphoto: Spiderstock, 8; Newcom: Swoan Paker/Reuters, 25, Brendan Bannon/Polaris, 11, Doug Benz/Reuters, 29, Ethan Hyman/Raleigh News & Observer/MCT, 21, Julia Wall/Raleigh News & Observer/TNS, 7; Rex Features: Jacob Kupferman/CSM, 27; Shutterstock Images: Fortyforks, 13, Jai Agnish, 5

Design Elements

Shutterstock Images: GraphicDealer

Printed in the United States of America.
032019 000073

TABLE OF

CONTENTS

NUMBER-ONE PICK TO SUPERSTAR

Sidney Crosby has been a hockey star since he was a young boy. He had a personal trainer by the time he was 14. By 15, hockey legend Wayne Gretzky called him "the best player since Mario Lemieux." When Crosby was 17, he signed a contract with Reebok worth $500,000. He had not yet played a single second of professional hockey in the National Hockey League (NHL). In 2005 he was drafted first overall by the Pittsburgh Penguins.

During the 2005–06 season, Crosby brought a lot of attention to the NHL with his incredible play and likable personality. More than a decade later, his jersey remains one of the most purchased by fans around the world. The superstar has set numerous NHL records. He has led the Penguins to three Stanley Cups.

Sidney Crosby has put in a lot of work behind the scenes to help him become one of hockey's biggest stars.

Crosby earns $4.5 million every year in **endorsement** deals with brands such as Gatorade and Tim Hortons. His commitment to training and recovery helped him get to where he is. When fans are not around, Crosby's teammates see how much effort he puts into every part of his practice. The superstar often stays behind after his teammates have left the ice to work on one more drill.

How do players like Sidney Crosby become superstars? What do they eat? How do they train and travel? Here's a sneak peek at what happens behind the scenes of pro hockey.

endorsement—a statement or advertisement in support of a product or service

WORKOUTS

Athletes work out for hours each week to reach their peak performance. NHL players focus on five main goals: speed, strength, **agility**, flexibility, and reaction time. They need to move fast to keep up with the speed of the game. They also need to stay strong to battle other players for the puck.

Conditioning coach Mike Kadar has worked for the Detroit Red Wings. Kadar likes to work out players' whole bodies to keep them in shape. Players do skater strides where they jump from side to side like they are ice skating. They also do lunges and squats to work out their lower bodies. Lifting weights strengthens the arms and shoulders. Holding weights while doing sit-ups on a medicine ball makes for strong and stable **core** muscles.

agility—the ability to move quickly and easily
conditioning coach—a coach who helps players exercise and build muscles
core—the muscles around the trunk of the body

Strength and conditioning coach Bill Burniston helps goalie Scott Darling do dumbbell presses.

In the off-season, players can do different exercises to stay fit, especially outdoors. Michael Grabner showed off his lower body strength in an online video of one of his workouts. Grabner stood waist-deep in a swimming pool near the edge. Then he jumped all the way out of the pool and landed on his feet on the concrete deck.

Medicine balls are padded balls that come in different weights. Players can use them for strength training.

Traditional workouts are not enough to keep an NHL player at his best. Conditioning coach Matt Nichol has worked with many NHL stars, including Taylor Hall, Mike Cammalleri, Tyler Seguin, and Wayne Simmonds. Nichol makes up new exercises to help with skills such as agility and reaction time. Nichol has players run laps together in a line while quickly tossing heavy medicine balls to each other. This helps players with **endurance**. It also helps players practice their awareness of the people around them. This is an important skill on the ice.

Nichol also likes to push his players by having them exercise in new ways. It may be hard to picture hockey stars doing ballet, but Nichol makes it part of his workouts. While ballet is very different from hockey, they both require **precision** and agility. These skills help with tasks such as shooting the puck and moving quickly on the ice.

endurance—the ability to keep doing an activity for long periods of time

precision—the ability to be very accurate or exact

GAME-DAY PREPARATIONS

Hockey players are busy on game day. In the morning, they meet at the arena for practice on the ice. The team does skating drills and takes shots on goal. Once the practice has finished, the players return to the locker room, where **media** members can join them for interviews. Here players answer reporters' questions about the team and the upcoming game.

Once the interviews are done, the players and coaches meet to discuss their opponent. They watch videos of the other team to prepare. In the afternoon, players return home or head to their hotels. Many take a nap to restore their energy. Then they go back to the arena, put on their gear, and do a short warm-up on the ice. Finally, the game begins.

media—TV, radio, newspapers, and other communication forms that send out messages to large groups of people

FAST FACT

During a game-day practice, a starting goalie will almost always leave the ice before the backup goalie. The second goalie will stay on the ice to get more practice.

Edmonton Oiler center Connor McDavid puts on his uniform, pads, and skates in the locker room.

FOOD AND FUEL

What do NHL players eat to stay healthy and fit? On game days, players like to stick with proteins and **carbohydrates**. Protein helps build muscle. Carbohydrates provide energy all day. Mark Scheifele begins his game days with a smoothie, eggs, and oatmeal. Pregame meals can be chicken, salmon, or **quinoa** with vegetables such as beets, broccoli, and asparagus. Postgame meals at the rink help with recovery and might be chicken or beef tacos.

Players are often strict about what they eat. Defenseman Niklas Hjalmarsson takes three weeks off at the end of the season to eat whatever he wants. After the three weeks are over, he goes back to his diet plan.

carbohydrate—a substance found in foods such as bread, rice, cereal, and potatoes that gives you energy
quinoa—a grain from South America

Meals high in protein and fiber, such as chicken and asparagus, can help players maintain energy levels.

Hjalmarsson eats steak for dinner every night when on his diet. He also drinks a lot of juice made from greens such as spinach, kale, and romaine lettuce.

FAST FACT

In the 2012–13 season the Chicago Blackhawks had their own secret recipe for a pregame and recovery drink. It included many fruits, vegetables, and herbs. The drink was developed to help players' performance during the long season.

SUPERSTITIONS

Many NHL players believe in **superstitions**. They are convinced that the tiniest things will affect their good luck. Some players' superstitions involve their sticks. Sidney Crosby's sticks must be cut to a certain length and taped a certain way. Karl Alzner, the Canadian defenseman for the Washington Capitals, taps his stick on the ice 88 times to the beat of the Canadian national anthem. Then he traces the outline of a maple leaf.

Superstar Wayne Gretzky refused to have his hair cut while the team was on the road. He was also superstitious about his drinks after warm-ups. He would drink a Diet Coke, water, Gatorade, and then another Diet Coke.

superstition—a belief that an action can affect the outcome of a future event

Once Sidney Crosby's sticks are taped, no one can touch them. If someone does, Crosby will re-tape the stick.

HANDS OFF!

A superstition held by players throughout the entire league involves the trophies for the Eastern and Western Conferences. It is considered bad luck to touch the trophies when they are presented to the conference champions. That's because they are not the trophy the teams want. Teams only want to hold the Stanley Cup. It's thought that touching the conference championship trophy will curse the team to only win that award and not the Cup.

CONTRACTS

A hockey player signs a contract when he joins a new team. The contract includes his salary, signing bonus, performance bonuses, and many other items. The amount of money an NHL player makes depends on many different things. Age, skill, how well he has played in the past, and personality all play a role. General managers look at these key issues to help decide how much to pay a player.

Players under the age of 25 are signed to a two-way entry contract for up to three years. "Two-way" means that at any time, the NHL team can send the player to the club's minor-league team in the American Hockey League (AHL). Players are usually sent down to gain more experience and playing time.

K'Andre Miller signed a two-way entry contract with the New York Rangers after being drafted in the first round in 2018.

After a player's entry contract expires, he becomes a restricted free agent. His current team has a window of time to sign him to a new deal. If that deadline passes without the two sides reaching a deal, another team can offer him more money. However, his current club can match the offer to keep him. If his team doesn't, he is free to sign with any club. Players become unrestricted free agents after playing for seven years or when they turn 27. As unrestricted free agents, they can sign with any club.

Trades

Players can be traded any time during the season until the trading deadline in late February. It can be an exciting time for fans, but the players often feel differently.

Trade deadlines can be stressful for players as teams **negotiate** by phone to work out the details. When a player is traded, his family may choose to stay behind in the old city until the season is over. Then they might move after the season. Because of the stress trades can cause, many star players have no-trade clauses negotiated into their contracts. There are two types of no-trade clauses. With a complete no-trade clause, the player can't be traded. With a limited no-trade clause, the player has approved a list of teams for trades.

negotiate—to bargain or come to an agreement with someone else

FAST FACT

Most teams don't trade their best player. The Oilers' trade of Wayne Gretzky to the Los Angeles Kings in 1988 is considered the most shocking swap in NHL history.

General Manager Dale Tallon (right) introduces newly traded Roberto Luongo to the Florida Panthers at a press conference.

Many NHL teams believe in locking down their star players to long contracts when they are still relatively young. Sidney Crosby, Alexander Ovechkin, and Steven Stamkos still play for the same teams they signed with as **rookies**.

rookie—a first-year player

ENDORSEMENTS

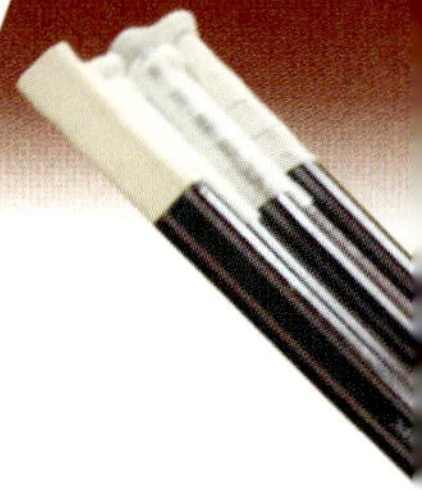

Famous athletes often make money by advertising products. The biggest stars get the largest contracts, both on and off the ice. Businesses want the most famous players to advertise what they have to offer. When a company wants a certain player to endorse its product, it will call that player's agent. NHL players typically use the same agent for both team and endorsement negotiations.

Athletes can work with sponsors in many ways, from making appearances at events to having their picture used to advertise a product. Hockey equipment companies such as CCM and Reebok often advertise using NHL stars. Well-known Canadian brands such as Canadian Tire and fast-food restaurant Tim Hortons also use NHL players in commercials.

FAST FACT

As a child Sidney Crosby played in the Tim Hortons youth hockey program. It was called "Timbits." A Tim Hortons commercial shows a six-year-old Crosby skating in his Timbits jersey.

Eric Staal of the Minnesota Wild has an endorsement with ice hockey equipment manufacturer, Bauer.

LEARNING THE LANGUAGE

NHL players come from many countries around the world. These include Austria, Denmark, Latvia, and Switzerland, just to name a few. Some players coming into the NHL don't speak English. They may depend on other teammates from the same country who have already learned English. Veteran players can help teach the new players the language. Other players get help from tutors or take classes to learn the language.

When Russian superstar Evgeni Malkin became a Pittsburgh Penguin, he was very uncomfortable speaking English. Veteran Sergei Gonchar served as the rookie's **interpreter** with the media until he learned the language.

interpreter—a person who can tell others what is said in another language

FAST FACT

In 2018 the NHL had players from 17 different countries. With so many nationalities, some teams have found it easiest to make English the universal language of the team.

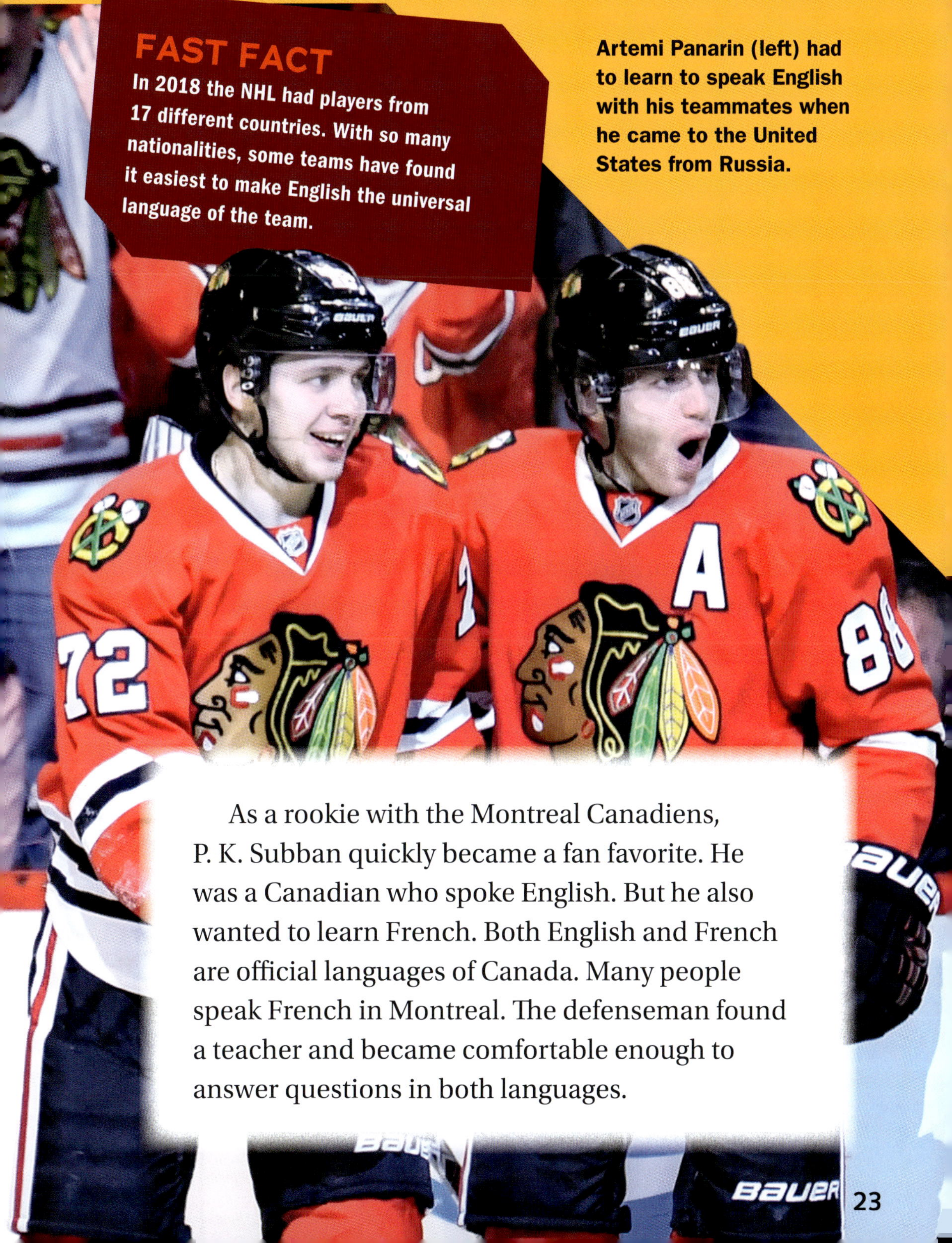

Artemi Panarin (left) had to learn to speak English with his teammates when he came to the United States from Russia.

As a rookie with the Montreal Canadiens, P. K. Subban quickly became a fan favorite. He was a Canadian who spoke English. But he also wanted to learn French. Both English and French are official languages of Canada. Many people speak French in Montreal. The defenseman found a teacher and became comfortable enough to answer questions in both languages.

CHARITABLE WORK

The NHL works hard to give back to society. The entire league comes together to raise funds for charity. The Hockey Fights Cancer project is meant to unite hockey players in support of people fighting the disease. By 2017 the project had raised more than $18 million. The funds went toward cancer research, hospitals, and local charities throughout Canada and the United States.

FAST FACT

Although a labor dispute led to part of the 2012–13 season being canceled, NHL players made the most of their time off. They raised more than $1.8 million for charity by organizing and playing 10 exhibition games.

After a 2010 earthquake, P. K. Subban (left) and Georges Laraque spent time doing charitable work and playing hockey with children in Haiti.

Individual athletes also take up causes of their own. In 2014 Swedish brothers Henrik and Daniel Sedin created the Sedin Family Foundation. The twins spent their entire careers with the Vancouver Canucks. Vancouver is in British Columbia. The Sedin Family Foundation helps schools and community groups throughout the province.

In 2015 P. K. Subban became the biggest athlete donor in Canadian history. He gave $10 million to the Montreal Children's Hospital. Subban was traded to the Nashville Predators the following year. But he regularly returns to the hospital to visit patients and offer support.

LIFE IN THE AHL

The NHL's minor-league teams in the AHL have a mixture of young players and veterans. All are trying to make their way to the NHL.

The AHL is less profitable than the NHL. Players make less money and travel is less comfortable. AHL players travel largely by bus. They spend many hours cramped together with teammates while traveling. Some try to sleep, while others like to watch movies or TV shows. The bus rides can be uncomfortable, but the time spent together helps the players become close friends.

Older players try to teach the younger ones good habits such as eating right and showing up to meetings on time. They also put them to work in other ways. For example, rookies are in charge of keeping the bus clean.

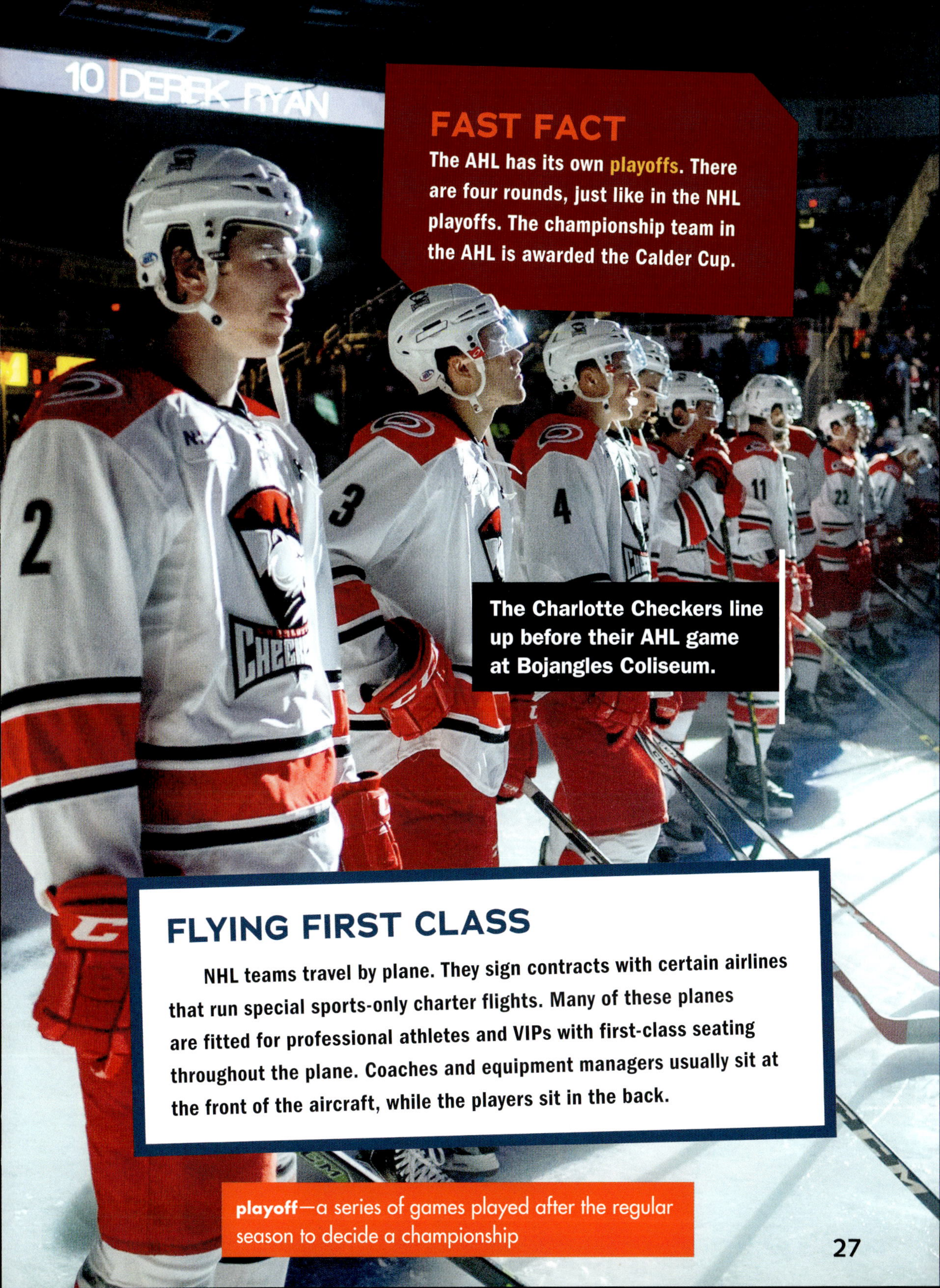

FAST FACT

The AHL has its own **playoffs**. There are four rounds, just like in the NHL playoffs. The championship team in the AHL is awarded the Calder Cup.

The Charlotte Checkers line up before their AHL game at Bojangles Coliseum.

FLYING FIRST CLASS

NHL teams travel by plane. They sign contracts with certain airlines that run special sports-only charter flights. Many of these planes are fitted for professional athletes and VIPs with first-class seating throughout the plane. Coaches and equipment managers usually sit at the front of the aircraft, while the players sit in the back.

playoff—a series of games played after the regular season to decide a championship

A DAY WITH THE STANLEY CUP

NHL teams play to become the Stanley Cup champion. But after a team wins the title, the Stanley Cup trophy doesn't sit in a case. Each player gets one day to spend with the trophy during the off-season. An employee of the Hockey Hall of Fame, called the Keeper of the Cup, always travels with the trophy. Almost all players like to bring the Cup back to their hometowns. Players show it off to friends and family. They have a lot of fun with it in the process.

FAST FACT

After winning the Cup in 2018, Washington Capitals captain Alexander Ovechkin had his picture taken in bed with the trophy.

Patrick Kane took the Stanley Cup to Niagara Falls to celebrate the Blackhawks championship in 2010.

Chicago Blackhawks star Patrick Kane brought the Cup to his hometown of Buffalo, New York, after the 2010 playoffs. He also took it to Niagara Falls and lifted the Cup under the waterfall.

Marian Hossa won the Stanley Cup three times with Chicago. He took the trophy back to his home in Slovakia. He ate pastries from the Cup each time.

Sylvain Lefebvre used the Cup during an important event with his family in 1996. The former Colorado Avalanche defenseman had his daughter **baptized** in the Cup.

baptize—to pour water on someone as part of a Christian religious practice

GLOSSARY

agility (a-JIL-uh-tee)—the ability to move quickly and easily

baptize (BAP-tize)—to pour water on someone as part of a Christian religious practice

carbohydrate (kahr-boh-HY-drayt)—a substance found in foods such as bread, rice, cereal, and potatoes that gives you energy

conditioning coach (kuhn-DISH-uhn-ing KOHCH)—a coach who helps players exercise and build muscles

core (KOR)—the muscles around the trunk of the body

endorsement (in-DORS-muhnt)—a statement or advertisement in support of a product or service

endurance (en-DUR-enss)—the ability to keep doing an activity for long periods of time

interpreter (in-TUR-prit-uhr)—a person who can tell others what is said in another language

negotiate (ni-GOH-shee-ate)—to bargain or discuss something to come to an agreement

playoff (PLAY-awf)—a series of games played after the regular season to decide a championship

precision (pri-SIZH-uhn)—the ability to be very accurate or exact

rookie (RUK-ee)—a first-year player

superstition (soo-pur-STI-shuhn)—a belief that an action can affect the outcome of a future event

READ MORE

Frederick, Shane. *Hockey's Record Breakers.* Record Breakers. North Mankato, Minn.: Capstone Press, 2017.

Lebrecque, Ellen. *The Science of a Slap Shot.* Full-Speed Sports. Ann Arbor, Mich.: Cherry Lake Pub., 2016.

Zweig, Eric. *Hockey Hall of Fame Heroes: Scorers, Goalies and Defensemen.* Hockey Hall of Fame. Richmond Hill, Ontario: Firefly Books, 2016.

INTERNET SITES

Use FactHound to find Internet sites related to this book.

Visit *www.facthound.com*

Just type in this code: 9781543554267

INDEX